Fathom

JENNY LEWIS trained as a painter before reading English at St Edmund Hall, Oxford and gaining an M.Phil in Poetry from the University of Glamorgan. She has been a singer–songwriter, an advertising copywriter, a children's author, playwright and screenwriter, a teacher and a civil servant. She lives in Oxford and teaches poetry at Oxford University.

To my father, Thomas Charles Lewis

JENNY LEWIS

Fathom

Oxford*Poets*

CARCANET

First published in Great Britain in 2007 by
Carcanet Press Limited
Alliance House
Cross Street
Manchester M2 7AQ

A CIP catalogue record for this book is available from the British Library
ISBN 978 1 903039 81 6

The publisher acknowledges financial assistance from Arts Council England

Typeset by XL Publishing Services, Tiverton
Printed and bound in England by SRP Ltd, Exeter

of his bones are coral made

Ariel's song, Act I, scene ii, *The Tempest*

Acknowledgements

Some of these poems, or versions of them, have appeared in or been performed at:

I Am Twenty People! (Enitharmon 2007), *Oxford Poets 2000* (Carcanet Press), *The Oxford Magazine*, *The Reader*, *Poetry Now*, *Iota*, *The Frogmore Papers*, *Poetry Direct*, *the magazine* and *The Exeter Prize Anthology*. 'Epilogue', 'Troubadour' and 'Perfect' are from *The Art of Loving Honourably*, performed with the early music group Third Voice at several festivals and at the Royal Festival Hall. 'Those birds fly well' and 'Come to me my beloved' are from *Garden of the Senses*, jointly commissioned by the *Sunday Times* Oxford Literary Festival 2005 and the Pegasus Theatre, Oxford; earlier versions appeared in *Other Poetry 2004*. 'In the Blood' is part of a poetry cycle commissioned by Mediva for the Brighton Early Music Festival 2005.

Thanks to Stephen Knight and the University of Glamorgan; my sister Gillian Beetham; Yasmin Sidhwa and Euton Daley; Mimi Khalvati; Claire Crowther; Lucy Newlyn, with whom I ran the Synergies Creative Writing workshops at Oxford; Joe Butler, Oliver Mantell and Bruno Guastalla; Tinker Mather; Peter Mortimer and Valerie Laws; Jerry Biers; Ann Allen and Clare Norburn of Mediva; Angie Prysor-Jones and Sally Dunsmore; and especially to Keiren Phelan and Arts Council South East for their support, including grants to work with the Pegasus Theatre, Oxford and to study troubadour lyrics in the Languedoc in 2001.

Contents

Woman Brushing Her Hair

after Degas

In spring, I lived underwater with it –
my dappled hands held auburn hanks
like uncoiled ropes to brush and brush
while my thoughts drifted upwards
into the pearly green and umber.

By summer, my face was a scribble –
no eyes, a mute mouth, I forced the auburn
from its lair at the nape of my neck,
brushed it over my brow in torrents
with hands like ham bones: by now
I knew I couldn't tame it by myself.

That autumn, I sat on a bed while my maid
tried to groom it. *Does it hurt?* she asked,
as the auburn itself fell like a curtain
over any other possibilities my life held;
she tilted her head and pulled, spilling
a ginger snakeskin over my face and forearms.

In winter, roasting chestnuts, I was caught
in the blaze, my dress became flames,
my maid grabbed the inferno and tried
to brush it out; a jigsaw of shapes held us firmly
in place while in one corner, just in the picture,
a dab of dappled pearl.

Sur Le Pont des Arts

He's looking at a painting of a river and trees,
houses roughly charcoaled in against a foggy smudge,
a foreground blob that could be a terrier's shadow

or a black hole of invisible light, dark matter
sucking viewers into the artist's untidy mind,
showing them the dissatisfied wife left clearing plates

after a silent Sunday lunch, the son who bores him,
the treasured daughter who ran off to the Pyrenees
with a specialist in sustainable energy

who builds houses out of cartons and solar panels,
where rotas of guests are needed so that they can pee
frequently in order to keep the bathroom lights on.

He's looking at a painting of a river and trees
and thinking about his mistress whom he hasn't seen
for three weeks because she's gone to stay with a sister

he knows she's just invented; now he's thinking about
his new hat, a smart homburg, and how superior
it is to the artist's floppy hat which is hiding,

probably, a mess of impasto passing for brains;
he's thinking of the terrier, who has just caught up
and is now regarding him with small, adoring eyes.

He's thinking it costs him more to feed the terrier
than buying the new homburgs he prefers to his wife.
He's thinking his mistress is a liar, the artist

is an impostor, the artist's wife and son should leave,
the artist's daughter and her husband are complete fakes
and that his own wife is less attractive than a hat.

He's thinking that his terrier is an expensive
excrescence; in fact, he's wishing he was someone else.
He's looking at a painting of a river and trees.

10

Swan

Consulting the bones, no one could have
predicted it, except that the dull roar
of the ring-road, constant as toothache,
drowned out a sound, the drumming of wings
on up to the lock where the year turned
fiery amber in the beaten sheet of river:
the sky, rolling away, showed its wild
markings like a shoal of bloodied mackerel
dumped over the side

and none noticed the silent creature
mourning the death of its mate, heading away
from the city where thousands of TV screens
made a babel of sound out of light.

Hare

They made new forms and in them rested
words, then watched them bolt and spring
in ways Taliesin might have dreamed of:

some spoke in colours deep as Arles
lavender, others were held by hawks
which circled over gorges, rose and rose
in fractured slipstreams, spoke in tongues
which changed our thoughts for ever.

One Easter, I was sitting by a stream,
my feet in splashing water, facing the April sun,
when a hare came and laid down with me

as if instructed to: while I wondered
at this, I heard, in the next field, a lamb,
ignorant of its message, begin to bleat.

Those birds fly well which have little flesh

Although it is not in the rules,
she tests herself, leaving the bread
and cheese untouched until her maid
takes it away; and the more she hungers
the more she has to test herself

she is not allowed to beat herself,
to flail herself with nettles
or hedgehog skins – the abbot forbids it

she is not allowed to cut herself,
but she can force herself to lie
on stones until the imprint on her body
is like a nail in her side

she can force herself to sit, undressed
under the window on winter's nights
until her bones groan with cold –

if she doesn't eat, her body will remain
pure and empty to receive the sacrament

the wafer is like honesty, a paper moon,
and she is a fledgling stretching up its beak
to take the gift, turning the web of her blood to silver:
her flesh thin as air.

Come to me my beloved, my bright bride

At first she seems to be drowning
      her self diffusing
like pigment in water

then she feels she is melting
      a fire outside and in her
white as an orchard in blossom

at last she knows
      the melting is blood
as red as her own

her senses are five birds
      her eyes become doves
to approach him

when she herself is the city
      she is filled with music
which is the food of heaven

now she is a garden of scents
      she is a flower opening
in her bridegroom's heart

Fathom

My face
is changing again

I caught it in a different light
yesterday

the flaky grey
of ocean-going
tankers

my face has turned
to someone else's

inside the inside
of the ocean, fish are hanging
cuttle-coloured

they sway, silent
not even a rattle of bones

and the dead stir in us too,
coming as they do from the weight
of darkness

they want our breath

want to tunnel out of us,
force apart our gullets,
appear stark-white

and raving at daylight

one more moment
they plead
just one more.

One More Moment

They're shouting from bone,
antlers reared to the roof, and in front
a xylophone of ribs

the one nearest has a dashed-away
look to its skull, there are bits missing
but still it glares from haunted sockets

draws back non-existent lips to roar
the non-sounds gather somewhere dense
like light trying to lift itself:

this motionless stampede of creatures,
giraffe, moose, elk, llama – they could
be asking the questions we ask

why did you make us of flesh?
why not bronze or gold?
why put us here at all if not to last?

They Want Our Breath

We think we know that space is silent,
only the words of astronauts reach us
as they stumble as if through water to place
flags while all the time light is escaping
faster than the fastest sandstorm.

Here, the light is full of water, a membrane
of unshed rain, the sky a cheap pendant
you might wear round your neck for love,
the weight of it against your skin, as we,
stumbling home from the fair that time, felt
something pressing on us, invisible, silent:
the moon inside us, using up our breath.

Something Pressing

Summer comes, soft-footed to the doorway,
slips over the sill, threadless and shining,
filling us again with the old yearning,
making us want to skip work for the day:

high in the Altai, Umai shakes her grey
tattooed leather free from ice, and turning
in her grave gives off a smell of burning,
Kali is also on the move, they say:

meanwhile, on Jupiter, the mean wind-speed
is three hundred and thirty miles an hour –
a storm the size of Earth which shows up red

on NASA's screens: and, far from Ganymede,
Callisto, the most similar to our
own life-giving planet, is (already) dead.

Balcony

The daffodils had sooty trumpets
like herald angels from the poorer part
of heaven: our granny planted them

with bulbous winter fingers
around Christmas; she told us stories
about Lazarus and Nazarenes

and Gaderene swine falling from cliffs,
she said *hark!* instead of *listen!*
and *you can't make a silk purse*

out of a sow's ear. No! I said
It would be cruel to the sow:
she didn't hear.

Hark! Hark! The Lark! sat open
on the old German piano with its
scuffed legs and treacly varnish.

Your Tiny Hand is Frozen
on the wind-up gramophone
sounded like an asthma attack

until it got going; sometimes I hid
behind the daffodils to catch sounds
as they came up: a girl my age

down the road sat at her window
like a smudge in a painting book;
her mother fell down once with bags

full of empties like jingle bells:
another time some boys came round
the corner shouting –

*Christ I need a fuck! My balls
ache!* My granny was sleeping,
I put on *Jerusalem the Golden.*

Chair

You still see their products in showrooms,
sporting velvet or paisley, saved by the salesman
for the end of his spiel – the coup de grâce
and of course there's always the Parker Knoll.

She'd survived widowhood, bankruptcy,
and bringing up grandchildren until well into her eighties,
but finally my grandmother ran out of steam –
was reduced to sitting all day every day

with a pile of thrillers from Hammersmith library,
waiting for the health visitor, the district nurse,
old Mrs Hammond who did for us on Wednesdays.
The least we could do was provide a good chair.

I've finally thrown it out: threadbare,
full of moth, springs sticking through like ribs
of famine victims – it sits alone in the road
waiting for skip robbers or men from the council.

Bright Morning

for Tom

Coming into the bright morning as he used to,
quietly, feeling his way round the edge of silences,
appearing suddenly in doorways, smiling,

he witnessed scenes Vermeer could have painted –
a child stripping redcurrants, a woman with a letter,
a cat cleaning its paw, a man drinking from a pint pot:

now he says he watched it all as if from a distance,
like looking through a fishbowl at potbellied colours
and shapes bleeding sideways – the child at the window,

the woman crying, the man turning away; and inside
him, none of the brightness he brought to them,
but only despair and coldness, like a moonstone

where his heart should have been. He preferred
the garden, looking over the valley with its boundless
moments, its possibilities lying thick as grass stems

for him to chew over. His dens had entrances
only a small child could get through, and there he hid –
behind the old milking parlour, under the laurel,

between the holly hedges, in the drapes of the willow.
Is that where he transports himself to now? – away from
the grey and black of Manchester, the concrete stairwells,

the bad trips, the broken, the dying, the empty cans,
the kicked dogs? Or is it possible he feels
this life's at least more honest than those childhood

tableaux, and if he could look again, would he trample
down the barriers, and stampede through to this bright morning
where the pictures have, at last, been turned to the wall?

Drummer

for Ed

Your teacher showed me, once,
some pages of your hurried writing,
where, beneath the blots and squirls, we found
a slipstream of thought, weaving words
and spaces into an intricate rhythm section.

Just as now, with closed eyes and averted face,
you start to tease a beat from somewhere,
subtle as photons brushing skin:

it's your new mode of communication,
leading us a dance of sound, syncopated,
charismatic – like the way you wore
your short-brimmed hat of Symi straw,
exactly placed, insouciant, original.

Leaving

for Tom and Ed

I walk into empty rooms
where you once were, and you
once were

feeling the air for imprints
I want to pull that air round me,
like a shawl, for comfort

knowing the way it clung
round you both and how you wore it
like cloaks of sea, flickering lights

at its edges, or tiny fish
falling in a tremulous harvest
before disappearing:

there was always light
where you were, bowling across lawns
illuminating the dark days

around Christmas and long nights
when, on the hard-shouldered horizon,
other women's sons were tossed

by storms, had mothers
lighting candles for them,
for their safe return.

Child

A child, standing at an open window,
watching daylight fade and lights come on
along the seafront and the twinkling pier:
the Swanee Minstrels sing about Dixie,
she doesn't want the show to end.

She can sing all the songs, do all the actions,
pretends she has a black face and hands
sticking out from her Wincyette pyjamas:
Now get into bed her mother says,
Just five more minutes the child pleads.

Stop the minutes trickling light away,
the pier lights are like a twinkling necklace,
she imagines night wearing a necklace of lights
like a black mammy stooping down to her
with soft hands the colour of coal dust.

You must go to bed now her mother says,
she will kiss her goodnight and close the door:
then the others will come, stooping from corners,
she will hear their breathing like waves breaking,
the man with sand feet trickling away –

small, mean ones with gritty shell faces. The kiss
her mother gives her is like a butterfly on her cheek,
she imagines its wings, like powdered rainbows,
outside the Swanee Minstrels take off their black.
On the shore sweet-papers rock in the moonlight.

Mother

The scented air stooped round her shoulders
like the Jaeger scarf, when she brushed her blonde hair,
to keep her navy suits shipshape for business:

sunlight in squares as shiny as toffee
dusted the cut-glass vase and library book,
the china animals, his sepia photo.

The cups of tea to cheer her up
always spilt, the surprise spoilt: treats,
like everything else, were rationed

except she always had fresh flowers,
freesias, daffodils, narcissi from the Scillies,
or his favourite – lilies of the valley

unpretentious, green and white, their perfume,
of gardens and summer days, faint as the writing
from the hospital bed with which he pencilled
his last words of love.

Father

You were my father, but also the dead hero,
the young South Wales Borderer who led his troops
across the Mesopotamian desert, guided by stars.

We watched a silent film of mum, trim
in her Windsmoor tweeds, carrying into big close-up
armfuls of bluebells for you, smiling.

I'm glad you were my dad, but your dying meant
the nearest we got to sand was a borrowed flat in Hastings,
the nearest we got to bluebells was on Mother's Day at Kew.

Orphan

May our daughters be as the polished corners of the Temple

We knelt beside our iron beds to pray
to gentle Jesus meek and mild who held
a lamb and a lantern to comfort us:
and in assembly, in our blue serge tunics
and blazers with Masonic badges, we sang
of the Carpenter of Nazareth who stands
close by the heedless worker's side,
head bowed, showing his pierced hands
for which we, somehow, were made to feel
responsible. Just as our fathers' deaths –
when we failed to learn our logarithms –
were laid, mysteriously, at our door:
although we knew it couldn't be right
and our mothers' grieving, not our fault.

First Day

That first term she walked away
into the fog, down drooping avenues
of love-lies-bleeding, saying, later, that
she couldn't turn to wave because of tears:
not wanting to believe she really meant
to give me up, I tried to follow, struggle
from the grip of strangers – Matron
and Headmistress – and inside me, a shift
of atoms, clustered round a pole of darkness,
bent themselves along the warp my mind
made leaning after her; fog seeped
into my bloodstream, and the space
between us turned to no-man's-land.

School Drill

The Lower Playing Fields were out of bounds,
the bell from the Science Quad chimed seven,
small girls paraded soiled sheets with shame:
cloud shadows spread over the rounders pitch.

I wasn't chosen to be the point of the compass,
instead, a younger girl, with ramrod back, her heels
rapping over the parquet, led the formation
of wheeling girls representing the mason's art.

Orphaned children dressed in post-war drab,
utilitarian, as we were told our lives should be,
marching to *Colonel Bogey* and the *Dambusters*,
raised arms to our benefactors in dumb salutes.

Boarder

Each night I dreamed I was going home,
following my plait down to the train station,
trains whizzed past in their streaming hair of wind,
too fast to catch, and disappeared into the night.

The tunnel stretched out as far as London,
to the mansion flat with engraved glass on its door,
through it I saw the shadow of my grandmother,
approaching slowly, bent by patterns.

If only my grandmother would reach the door
I could go inside and be safe with my mother:
but the ringing was the school handbell. I woke
cold, curled like a cockle, hair newly shorn.

Character Forming

The girl in the next bed rocked herself
on and on, like a boat tethered in a cold
harbour: she couldn't spell, and was labelled 'thick'
but was rarely picked on and seemed to have the gene
that makes some people un-bullyable.

Perhaps it was because she drew for us
Snow White and the Seven Dwarves,
expertly sketched, with each character
recognisable as we were: Grumpy, Doc,
Sleepy, Happy, Bashful, Sneezy, Dopey.

Prospects

We lay, a dormitory of ten year olds, deciding
which death would be preferable:

Burning from the feet up like Saint Joan
would be worst, someone suggested.
You'd faint before it got too bad – the sturdy girl
cut out to be a nurse assured us.

Yet drowning would be just as horrible
we knew from when we held our breaths
in swimming, buoyant underwater on our silver strings
of seed pearl bubbles.

Worst of all, perhaps, a Viking burial –
scratching at rock until the air went
and us, with our unused breasts and wombs,
buried screaming with the old, dead king.

Survivors

She says the coldness of the water shocked her,
standing thigh-deep in the canal at midnight,
a duffle coat being the most moisture-absorbent thing
you could possibly wear when trying to drown yourself.

She talks, almost jovially, about how it was too shallow,
how silly of her to think this time she'd succeed:
the woman whose garden it was came out to ask *why?*
then wrapped her in blankets to await the ambulance.

All I can say is *you shouldn't have done it*, knowing
she's likely to try it again, and I will remember that day
at school, when the two of us moped homesick by the pond,
which looked the colour of twice-used bathwater

and suddenly I snatched off her hairband and ran away
then floated it far out among the reeds and water weed;
she followed slowly with her face down-turned
and I had no answer when she asked me *why?*

Lupins

for R

Lupins with their peppery, summery smell,
filled the brimming moment to its rim,
lifting the shadow my father left by dying:

eight years of living with my mother's grief
wiped clean by the heat and promise of the day,
and I, a small child, tending my garden

shedding the past for that moment's clarity,
absorbed and delighted by the task's simplicity,
planting stones in a rough circle, turning up worms

the colour of corsets, hardly aware that time
was passing, the smell of gym shoes
and grass being cut, or the way the heavy

summer air curved the sound
of four o'clock striking.

Now, lupins always remind me of you,
how you lifted the stain of childish sorrows,
kept the day bright like a sun-warmed garden

until night came and our spirits ventured –
silently, hand in hand, without fathers:

black as lupins at dusk
setting out against a tall sky.

Secret

You were my secret pleasure and my consolation,
you filled the place left empty by my father's death
and warmed the torn-off parts of me that felt the cold
so badly, all those years ago at boarding school.

No one else could comfort like you did, your soft voice,
your dark obliterating body. You were my ashlar and my compass,
still rooted in your own culture where spirits took tea with aunts
on porches, summoned by a chicken's fluttering corpse.

You told me once your mother broke stones by the road
for a living, you told me she spat saliva in your mouth
to bind you to her, sharing slave blood, passing on to you
that same fierce, human grip on life she had.

Beside you I felt weak and pale – the way I gave up
so easily, the way I stood aside and let other people
take from me: easy come, easy go for us who never
had to fight for the right to be.

Aubade

I thought of bread and butter sliced thin;
a brown egg, smooth as a knuckle;
a cup of milk, slightly warmed
already forming a brave, new skin.

Then later, chocolates, sweet wine,
maraschino cherries shiny in syrup
reflecting panes of brightness; cream
whipped to an adolescent frenzy.

But, lying there with you, the dawning light
seemed, so far, painless. I waited for you to wake
with appetite refreshed by sleep, knowing
what you enjoyed most was my hunger.

Tasting Notes

Traces of spice lingered on my palate
long after the smoky day had ended:
your body of dark plum and liquorice –

a bowl of Morello cherries bursting
with juices, while mine, flat and English,
needed notes of rose and burnt caramel

under the knees and along the cheekbones
to put life into it. Yet when night came
and you were reduced to highlights

I became the flinty splash of a stream
vaulting mountain passes – all that pale fire
you loved, brought alive by the moon.

Epilogue

You had to mind
a baby, once –

a fractious,
grizzling creature

that had caused its parents
weeks of sleepless nights

your method
was to put some music on
then lie down on the floor

and hold the baby
to your chest

where
like a tiny castaway
on a warm island

with limbs relaxed
and every spasm
of colic gone

it slept, soothed
by your breathing:

how I envied it,
and any other child

that had
such consummate
fathering.

Drunken Shadows

after Li Bai

Alone on the hillside, I raise my glass to the moon,
the sea in the distance swallows and sucks stones,
the wine in my mouth tastes of stones and shadows,
I think of court life and banishment.

A poem is like the tang of willow, carried
on the breeze through the windows of a wine lodge:
the smell of sedge as the evening darkens,
the heron's legs like broken stalks.

Once I wore jackets embroidered with peonies,
carried gardens on my back of silver and jade,
then they closed the great carved doors against me,
sent me to try my luck among beggars.

If I had a coin for every time I looked at the moon
I wouldn't be now just a penniless moon-gazer
who raises his glass alone on the hillside
while words lurch inside like drunken shadows.

Persephone

To start with, it was just a feeling in the bones
that I would like it down here, be at home
in the substructure of granite, basalt and ore.

Now I enjoy ordering the petrifaction
of gems to wear in my ears and on my body
emerald, amethyst, jacinth, zircon.

There's no liquidity, no constant movement
as up there, of clouds and oceans and no
expectations of me to be the light-giving

daughter of a goddess to whom people bow.
I can turn my attention to darker things, while
sticking pins in the cells of my pomegranate.

Cassandra

She woke in a nest
of shifting colours: half-tones
slithered round her neck

trying to enter
her and their blunt, waving heads
sprouted sheaves of words

she closed her ears to:
but her eye, her inner eye
saw red as Troy burned.

A Night with Ulysses

Winged back, scapulae like sails,
bones found in a desert bleached dry:
or a frail craft setting out, the bang
of its rigging strumming like wires.

You showed me a healed scratch
where Calypso caught you with her sharp nails
and intimate small wavings – those sirens
threw a rope of song that couldn't hold you.

Scylla and Charibdis clashed over you
but lost you: as for your tapestry
of quick conquests – your wife is already
losing the thread.

But now it's my turn to make fables,
wondering how far I'll go this time,
when the tide is going to turn,
watching for the ebb: no other reason.

Tribute

They made shields from themselves, a phalanx of bony mantles
we crushed as we stepped ashore: clams, cockles, whelks – oysters
that changed from male to female over a hundred tides.

Then those women with their blue-veined forearms flung back
against the pebbles, not understanding us – their men off fighting
somewhere behind the hills, lost in perpetual drizzle and cloud.

All we wanted was comfort, but they showed us no compliance,
instead, they shut their ears to the foreign sounds we made,
white ears more delicate than shells, with tiny, labyrinthine cochleas.

They were less impressive than African bounty – the conch
and cowrie we used as currency, displays of wealth to string
round the necks of our black-haired Pompeian women.

We took them anyway, translucent as the sunlight our ships turned
to plough through: scant booty, but it was enough for Caligula.

In the Blood

As we went walking by the edge of the ocean
the river lay haphazard in the creek like an eased-off dress
and the church on the headland was a prow

I felt the current running, the undermovement,
and the mist above it snagged by the sea's chainmail surface

and I said *if you go your ship will be a fragment of the world*
cast adrift and because we can't tell where you begin and I end,
if you go, a part of me will be cast adrift from itself

      but already the wind
smelling of salt and sea wrack, brought images of shoals
plunging like arrows

            and he needed to be there, at the helm, heaving
hearts of oak into the headwind, skippering
      forests towards horizons

feeling the slick of the wind, the slide of the deck

the setting out and coming back
feeling the slack

ropes smelling of tar and brine

for as much as *I* was in his blood
so was the roving life, the gull's calls, the first mate's shouts
land ahoy, come about, look lively, hoist the mainsail

      and the languages they sailed through
that met them in succulent gusts – *ciao, bonjour, guten tag*
the boy heaving nets in the harbour, the cockle girl
with the gleaming eye

      adiós, au revoir, goodbye.

Piano

The only tunes she knows she learns by heart
crochets and quavers in a stream of notes
that gather pace into a dance of hands
and tumble through the dusty London flat
out over balcony railings, moving
beyond the houses to the green where keys

of linden spiral down. The sound of keys
in the lock – half day Wednesday – the girl's heart
lifts, she stops playing Barcarole (moving,
despite her two left hands and the wrong notes)
and hurries to the front door of the flat
to take a parcel from her mother's hands.

Her mother's hands and her grandmother's hands,
dressmakers, homemakers, holding the keys
to a childhood of shadowed rooms: the flat,
dimly lit, with austere kindness at heart,
creaks its timbers with long-suffering notes
like a house built on sand, always moving.

When her father died they came to this flat,
it had meant them packing up and moving
from a pretty terraced house in the heart
of a cathedral city; now *all hands*
on deck is the motto, one of the keys
to survival is to strike the right note

of pulling together, of taking note
of one's blessings, like this intriguing, flat
parcel her mother brings, putting her keys
away, closing the front door, and moving
to the kitchen where, with impatient hands,
the girl unwraps the ice cream; in her heart

she'd rather have her mother whose soft heart
knows that the child misses her, but a note
of gaiety! The ice cream is handed
round, striped like a deckchair, cut into flat
rainbow squares, and soon the child is moving
back to the piano's ivory keys

to play by heart for her mother, each note
lovingly learned, her hands over the flat
surface moving in search of the right keys.

Baboushka

Wherever the Trans-Siberian Express stops
there they are in their boots and headscarves
like shadow puppets against a pliant screen
of thousand-mile birch forests, pushed on
from the wings with trugs of home-made pies,
cold beer and chocolate to sell to travellers.

And the old woman on Komsomol Avenue
bent double by the weight of her shopping
scuttling along the tracks of the trolley-bus –
she looked like one of those matryoshkas
they sell for 200 roubles in Arbat Street
that get smaller and smaller as if receding

into history where small girls help collect
dewberries at their dachas: all that jam-making
for a teaspoonful of sweetness – these children
are brought up on grandmothers' sayings:
lie down with a dog, you'll get up with fleas,
the best way to get rid of work is to do it –

whatever else, Baboushka knows best, there's
comfort in that: just as my own grandmother told
the weather from a feeling in her bones, struggled
with us to the 'gods' at the Old Vic and Aldwych
to give us a taste of Shakespeare, gave herself
half portions so our plates could be full.

Pushkin Is Everything!

They told me it was a cleaning woman
who found Pushkin's statue, face down
in the mud in a frock-coat of leaves, red
and yellow with tongues of fire in them:

apparently, she tried to clean him up,
felt it was wrong to leave him, poor man,
but no one would help – his sort of thinking
wasn't wanted any more, it was about
the same time they started to arrest books.

At last they've reinstated him on his plinth
and made his stories into wrought-iron
wreaths in Pushkin Square, so students
meeting at the benches for coffee can say
once more *Pushkin is everything!*

David

His mind is a cathedral flooded with saints,
flaming crimson, gold, purple, magenta,
they stride through his days and nights
pointing fingers, admonishing him.

He hears their voices crackling in the wireless,
buzzing from radiators, trying to get through:
sometimes they sing down the telegraph wires,
strum them until they shriek skies of sound.

He tries to decipher their codes, but it's hard
with that bitch next door banging nails
into coffins all night: she even comes
into his head sometimes, won't leave him be.

He knows he's a bit odd, knows it started
the night his father grabbed a hatchet
and split his mother's skull like a walnut –
funny there was no blood.

Tomorrow at the day centre he'll be fed buns
by lady volunteers, amaze everyone
with his knowledge of advanced mathematics,
play Bach full volume on Vera's electric organ.

There's a new girl he likes – she has calm eyes
like ponds, a smiling face: then he remembers
the walk home, the icy roads even in summer,
the men waiting to paint lines over his shoes.

His mum bangs from the next door bedroom
Go to sleep David, it's past midnight!
David turns his face to the wall,
closes his eyes, waits for the voices.

Slag

Growing up in its shadow
seems its gritty dust
wants to get into her knickers
soils the armholes of her vests
even before she sprouts hair there:

summer evenings, coming up
through lakes of vetch and loosestrife,
air moist as cow's breath, smelling
of cud and fodder and her breasts swing
slow as an udder, making the boys gasp
and the girls run ahead to shouting distance.

Their dads were right, she gives
to the first who asks, buries her face
in the slack of their shirts, never hears
the tip begin to slide.

At the funeral they wear beads of jet
as is the tradition in the valleys,
coal black and hard as a set jaw,
a mark of respect for those who died.

The Other Wife

She used to enjoy summer but now it seems
the world is all dolled up and nowhere to go,
the big chestnuts have started to look blowsy,
nights too hot to sleep and mosquito bites
on her ankles and behind her knees.

He thinks of her as his second wife, he said
when he last saw her – that time before Easter –
and she felt pleased: this is the next best thing,
she can be her own mistress, independent,
except for Christmas, it isn't so bad.

She keeps herself busy, does the church flowers,
filling the nave with stocks and peonies, the peonies
lean out with their overloaded globes
catching the light like shiny new lipstick:
and at night the stocks pour out a scent

that laps under the church door, down the path,
climbs up the wisteria beneath her window
and enters her dreams where she seems to be
always counting, counting hours and days
and seeds falling from their bursting plush.

Inana

he fathered her
then left a void

planted a seed
in the dark but the womb
grew darker

his absence
a poison that ran
down the walls

like damp

seven times seven
she shed herself

arched backwards
hung from a hook
through her belly button

a flower of muscle
peeled from the entry point

and round the tip
a flesh cushion
covered in scales
to hide the wires

in a rush
she entered the light
eyes polished wet

leaped upstream
the hook embedded still:
unseen

Troubadour

Strings of gut stretched
to within a cat's whisker
of snapping resonate
under his sensitive fingers

as if brought alive
by a momentary breeze,
and after a supper of serrano
and sestinas, he slips away

up into the tower
lays his lute on the pillow
of a lady

who vibrates with sighs
caused by his touch

cries when he leaves
by the bedroom window
(even though the stairs
are deserted)

and next night, miles away
in another castle

he makes a villanelle about
how he'll have her
painted naked on his shield

so that in battle
he can die beneath her.

Perfect

A dual existence between matter
and spirit, poised in flight
like a bird beating its wings over water

against the sun's rays, feeling it better
to be translated into air, to fight
the dual existence between matter

and spirit with poverty, to batter
flesh into chastity, make it light
as a bird beating its wings over water

power of blossom and bloom to flatter
our senses with joy of touch, smell and sight
betrays every creature's need for matter

as well as spirit, for the pure creator
has a dark counterpart of equal might,
and the bird beating its wings over water

is like spirit trying to shatter
its vessel, reveal its light, give insight
into duality: spirit and matter –
a bird beating its wings over water.

First Light

all day it dropped
its concrete blocks
onto the city
 importantly
 turning its jib
 this way and that
with men rising up
in its gorge

all night the blackbirds
sang in the artificial day
of arc lights
 and it stayed still
 high above chimneys
 saying *Leadbitter*
stiff as a child pretending
to be a robot

did it look lonely?
was that why he wanted
to climb it?
 he might have made it
 if the wind hadn't
 shuddered the metal
nowhere to grip
and then the fall

into an old lady's
flower bed
glinting with
 February snowdrops
 white as the swan
 on its muscle of water
that slipped under the bridge
as the crane woke

Bell

Imagine the sound of a bell
in that medieval silence –
like a cloud of glass breaking
against the sides of the valley

before the ring-road roar, before
the hum of wires and fridges

the silence then was true
silence, the darkness was true
darkness, so that a candle,
on a still night, might be seen
for miles

imagine the moon and stars,
cut out of steel, striking sparks
from the infinite blackness

and you walking back
up that hillside, welcomed
by half-remembered shapes
of trees, a dog barks,
each note returned once

only that and the sound
of your own footsteps
loosening the scree, closing
the distance between yourself
and home.

New Year

for Joe Butler

The snap of ice under our tyres, freezing fog high in the mountains
and a buzzard, brooding on a wire, looking out across what we
                                                              saw –
fields with ragged hems, vineyards poorly tailored, lacking buttons.

It was no surprise, at St Hilaire, that the abbey door was bolted.
On it a friendly note from St Anselm – *When I despair I remember*
                                                        the friend
who is always with me – and in the cloister, a fountain playing to the
                                                  stones and air.

At midnight, we stood on top of a hill and saw shooting stars: no
                                                              bells,
just owls hooting and the crack of frosty undergrowth as mice and
                                                              foxes
went about their business, making tomorrow's tracks.

Walking Meditation

Before paper there was cloud, air, forest,
and the words we write, made with mind images
and minerals, graphite, something in the ground
reduced to a powder that blows away into cloud
air and forest. The nuns, robed in maroon,
write on cards, teaching us our meditations.

Desire is a torch we hold in our hands,
its flame burns us as we walk into the wind,
without desire we can free ourselves;
the nuns and monks put on their saffron robes,
they kneel before the statue of Buddha, chanting,
the Temple is light and scented by orchids.

We walk with our Teacher, holding hands
like children, and the children hold our hands
and walk with us, leading us and our Teacher
through the plum orchards, slowly, each step
is a meditation: we feel with the soles of our feet
the ground meet us with its powdered history.

Before sunrise, the great bell wakes us,
its sound rolls slowly round the lake,
we reach for our clothes, smooth our hair,
and still half asleep, we stumble to the Temple,
kneel together, begin to count our breathing:
we try to see the world with Dharma eyes.

Thousands of sunflowers raise their heads,
we walk up the path to the top of the mountain,
our Teacher tells us that our lives are like waves,
no birth or death, only altered states of being –
beside the lotus pond we watch our reflections
like clouds passing over the surface of the water.

Notes

Pages 13 and 14, 'Those birds fly well which have little flesh' and 'Come to me my beloved, my bright bride' are epigraphs from the early thirteenth-century *Ancrene Wisse* (A Rule Book for Anchoresses).

Page 18, 'Something Pressing': Umai is the Turkish goddess of reproduction who protects pregnant women and small children. Kali is the Hindu goddess associated with the ego, time and death.

Page 27, 'Orphan': 'May our daughters…' is the motto of the RMIG (Royal Masonic Institution for Girls).

Page 39, 'Drunken Shadows': Li Bai (AD 701–762) is one of the most admired Chinese poets. He fell from favour at court and was exiled to Yelang, but later pardoned. One of his best-known poems is 'Drinking Alone With The Moon'.

Page 44, 'In the Blood': 'A ship is a fragment of the world cast adrift' – Joseph Conrad.